America's Unsung HERO ...Our Hero

David Hall

Selma to Montgomery March Campsite One

Written by Michele L. Waters
Illustrations by Janine Carrington

America's Unsung Hero...Our Hero
David Hall - Selma to Montgomery March Campsite One

ISBN:978-0-9828670-9-9

Written by Michele L. Waters
Illustrations by Janine Carrington

This book is based on the wisdom and truths I have carried from my upbringing and life experiences, which were passed down to me by my parents, grandparents, aunts, uncles, and cousins.

Published by Crystall Clear Publishing
www.crystallclearpublishing.com

Acknowledgements

I would first like to acknowledge all of my aunts, uncles, cousins, and friends who shared stories about my grandfather. Thank you for your support, so that future generations will know the courageous act performed by David Hall.

I acknowledge my husband, daughter, son, and grandchildren, who have inspired me to write this book.

Deep gratitude to Deré Scott for her exceptional editing and thoughtful feedback, and to my eldest granddaughter, Jasmine, whose keen eye and enthusiasm as my junior editor made this project even more special.

Thank you in advance to all who will purchase, read, and share this book with children, adults, and/or organizations.

Jasmine sat at the table full of books, very concerned for a thirteen-year-old. She was a very studious, young girl, pushing herself to excel in all school subjects and spending most of her leisure time participating in academic competitions rather than playing games.

"What's with the long face?" Grandma asked.

Jasmine looked up and let out a long sigh. "I have to write a paper about a famous person for school. There are too many famous people to choose from. This will take forever."

Zaria, Jasmine's little cousin, ran up to Jasmine, "Hi Jazzy," and climbed onto the chair next to her, tapping on the computer as usual. Zaria was intelligent and tremendously observant for a five-year-old.

"No, this is important school work. I can't play with you now," Jazzy sternly announced. Zaria's entire face sank.

Grandma laughed, "Okay, come on over here," waving them towards the family room. Grandma sat on the couch while directing her two granddaughters to sit on the rug facing her.

Grandma pulled a large photo book from underneath the end table.

"Jasmine, do you know what an unsung hero is?"

Jasmine looked concerned, shaking her head. "No, what is an unsung hero?"

"An unsung hero is a person who achieved great things, and committed acts of bravery, or self-sacrifice, but was never celebrated or recognized," Grandma stated.

Grandma's eyebrow raised while leaning toward the two girls, "You see, we have someone in our family who did a courageous and extraordinary thing, but you will not find him in any of those books over there. However, he's our very own hero!"

Both girls' eyes stretched, "Who, Grandma? Who is our hero?" Jasmine asked.

Grandma smiled, "I'm going to tell you and show you our unsung hero." She pulled a photo from the album showing them a young, handsome man.
Zaria looked at her older cousin for an answer, but quickly noticed her cousin was just as confused as she was.

Jasmine finally blurted out, "Who is that?"

"This is your great-great-grandfather," Grandma said proudly. "His name was David Hall."

Jasmine's crooked face said, "What great thing did he do? Or brave thing?"

"I'm going to get to that, but first I want to tell you who he was to just our family, friends, and his community, okay?"

"Okay, Grandma," Zaria yelled, knowing this was story time.

Grandma began telling the story of her late grandfather to the two curious girls. "My granddaddy, David Hall, was born October 23, 1905, to Matthew and Pearlie Hall in Snowhill, Alabama. They were your great-great-great-grandparents. Jazzy, as soon as your PaPa saw you, he said you looked just like Grandma Pearlie."

"I know," Jazzy said. "You and Mommy told me."

"In 1931, Granddaddy married Channie Hicks, my grandmother who I never had the honor to meet. She passed away when PaPa was a little boy." Grandma's face dropped, but she continued quickly.

"In 1940, your great-great-grandfather and grandmother, David and Channie Hall, bought eighty-eight acres of land in Selma, Alabama. During this time, most black people in the South could not afford to buy their land, so they became sharecroppers."

"Sharecroppers?" Jasmine asked.

"Yes," Grandma said. "A sharecropper was a farmer who lived and worked on land owned by someone else—usually white landowners. Instead of paying cash rent, they had to give a portion of their crops as payment. The landowners controlled almost everything—the tools, the seeds, even the housing—and they often overcharged for supplies. That kept many Black farmers trapped in debt they could never escape."

"Why?" Zaria asked, frowning.

Grandma sighed. "Because it was the only way many families could have a place to live and grow food. Some white landowners took advantage of that, keeping the sharecroppers, mostly Black families, tied to the land generation after generation."

"Granddaddy Hall and Grandma Channie had nine children, of which two passed away at young ages. The children helped work on the farm before and after school." Jazzy's face crumbled in disgust.

"Yes. It was hard work. Your great-great-grandparents grew nearly everything they needed for their family's food and to sell to earn money.

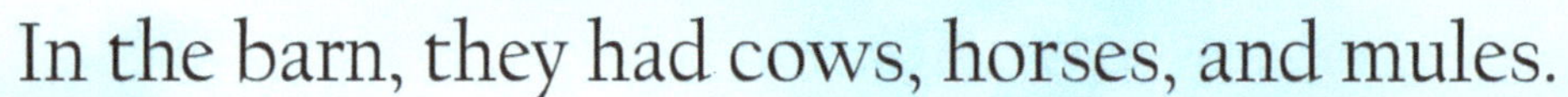

In the barn, they had cows, horses, and mules.

There was also a chicken coop full of chickens, hogs in the pig pen and plenty of goats roaming the land."

"Grandma, can we go to see the animals?" Zaria asked excitedly.

"I'm sorry, Zaria, but that was a long time ago. The land is still in our family, but it is not a working farm anymore."

"Every morning before sunrise, and again in the evening, the children, your PaPa, his siblings, and cousin Horace, when he lived there, would head to the barn to milk the cows. They'd clean the cow's udder, place a bucket underneath, and use a gentle squeezing motion to get the warm milk flowing. They would strain the fresh milk through clean cloths to remove any bits of hay or dirt."

"Ew!" the girls said in unison.

"Some milk was kept fresh for drinking, while they used some to make butter and buttermilk," Grandma proudly boasted. Cousin Horace told us how big his hands were and how strong he was now because of working on Granddaddy's farm.

The chicken coop was a busy place! Hens would lay eggs in straw-lined nesting boxes. The children's morning chores included gathering eggs in their baskets - carefully reaching under sitting hens who weren't always happy to share! They kept the coop clean with fresh straw and made sure the chickens had plenty of feed and clean water. The eggs were for baking cakes, scrambled eggs, pancakes for breakfast, or delicious biscuits."

A huge smile came over the girls' faces when Grandma mentioned some of their favorite foods.

"Keeping the chickens safe was a big job. Foxes would try to sneak into the coop, especially at night. Granddaddy built the coop strong, with wire mesh buried deep in the ground so foxes couldn't dig under. He made sure to lock the chickens in the coop every evening before dark. The family kept a good guard dog who would bark to alert them if any foxes came prowling around."

"I want a dog, Grandma," Zaria announced.

"You'll have to talk to your parents about that, Zaria," Grandma said.

"Yes, let's get back to the story," Jazzy impatiently stated.

"Another huge task was picking the cotton. I heard that Granddaddy's cotton field was massive, and guess who had to pick the cotton? His family."

"Grandma, I thought only slaves picked cotton."

"No, Jazzy, after slavery, Black people picked cotton to sell it for economic gain, just as the White people did. I will have to get into more details regarding the differences at a later date," said Grandma.

"Your aunts and uncles didn't just perform chores in the barn or chicken coop–your aunts had to sweep the dirt around the porch, on the porch, and from under the house."

"Wait, what?" Jazzy interrupted.

Grandma explained, "They didn't have pavement. They had to keep debris from around and under the house. Sometimes the chickens roamed under the house. Therefore, that area needed to be cleaned as well."

Jazzy let out a huge sigh.

"Living on a farm wasn't easy. Granddaddy taught PaPa and Horace how to hold the hogs down to put a ring through their strong, flat, shovel-like snouts to prevent them from pushing the dirt, called 'rooting' under the pens to escape.

One day, when Granddaddy was showing Horace how to perform this technique, the hog jumped loose and kicked Horace in the face."

Both girls looked shocked while Grandma burst into laughter.

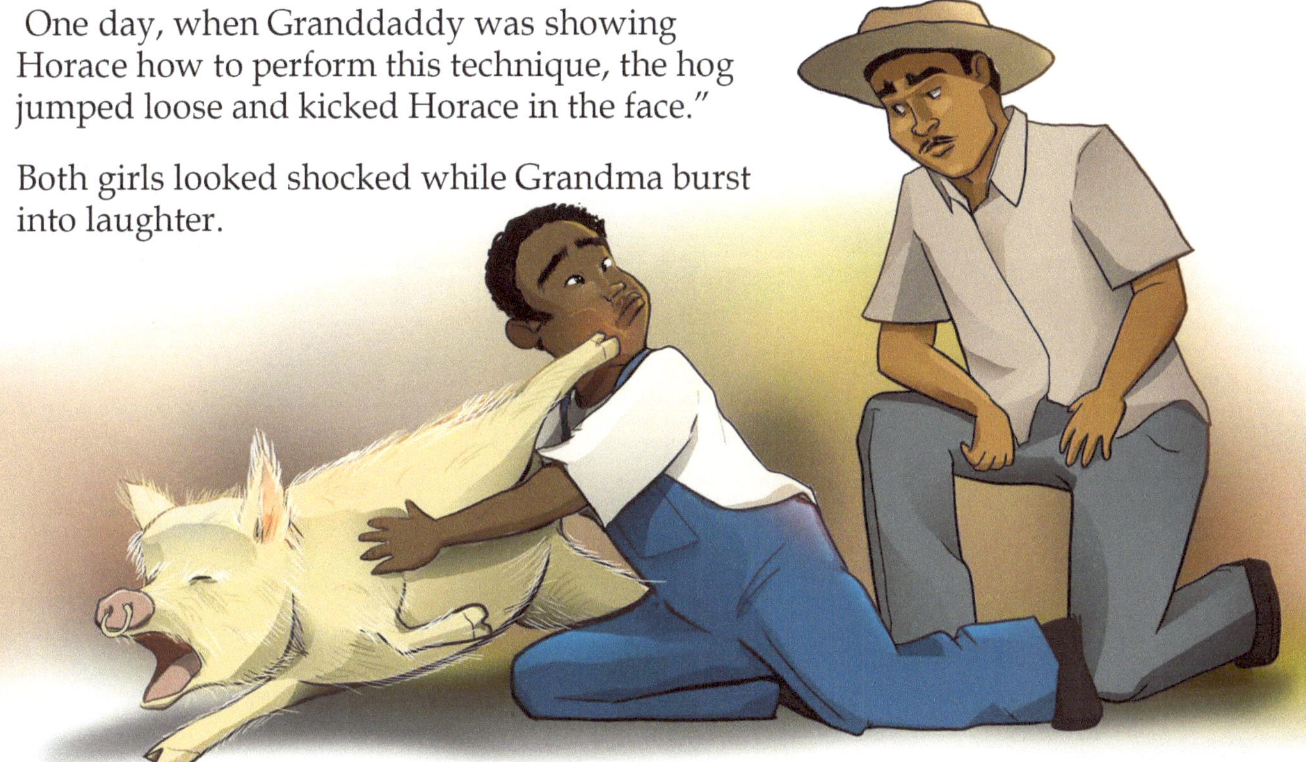

"Daddy told me how they prepared pork for the family. They raised hogs throughout the year, and in the cool winter months, would process the meat to make sausages, hams, and other cuts that could feed the family for many months ahead."

"Grandma, they raised the hogs to eat them?" Jasmine whispered, trying to spare her little cousin from that truth.

"Yes, Jasmine. However, you must understand that when we eat meat today, an animal has to be killed for us to consume it. That was how they survived back then, but now not everyone eats meat." Grandma winked.

"Besides the animals, our family grew plenty of vegetables like peas, greens, and fields of corn. Your great-great-granddaddy didn't depend on others to take care of him or his family, and he taught all of his children to rely on themselves and their abilities."

Grandma smiled. "He also planted a grove of pecan trees."

"Pecan? What's a pecan?" Jasmine asked.

"Pecans are nuts, like peanuts and almonds."

"Ugh, we don't like any kind of nuts, Grandma, but please continue." Jasmine waved for her grandma to move on.

***

"While the family worked the farm, my granddaddy also worked as the manager of maintenance for the GWC, George Washington Carver, housing authority, which was next to a church called Brown Chapel. Remember the name of that church," Grandma said while pointing at Jasmine. "You'll hear it often."

Jazzy gave a thumbs up.

"Granddaddy was a man of faith. He raised his family in the church. He instilled a strong work ethic in his children by example. He didn't just tell his children to work; he worked beside them, teaching them while working together. He was a man of few words; he allowed his actions to speak for him. His family could depend on him for assistance, if needed. He was also known to help others outside of his family, a friend and supporter to all who were in need. He was also known to assist people who lived in the projects where he worked - he was stern but had a big heart."

Grandma gently closed and opened her eyes. "I saw him as a gentle giant. I remember when we used to go to Selma every summer as children. Your Uncle Ron and I would love to go to the farm. I would run up to Granddaddy Hall to hug him. He always seemed to be sitting in this wooden chair right next to the front door when we got there. Then I would take off running to chase the ducks.

Grandaddy would let your Uncle Ron ride on the horse as his older cousin pulled him, but I was too small, I guess. I don't really remember why I couldn't ride the horse. My brother would also go to the pond to fish. I was scared to go to that pond because I thought a snake might get me.

The entire family would gather and have watermelon-eating contests. In my eyes, it was the biggest and best playground ever. There was so much peace, love, and excitement on the farm."

“You got a chance to see the animals,” Zaria pouted.

“Yes, some,” Grandma released a big sigh, “Moving forward....There was a time when Black Americans had to organize meetings and marches to end racial discrimination and gain equal rights under the law. This was called the Civil Rights Movement. It began in the late 1940s and ended in the late 1960s. Jazzy, do you know what discrimination means?”

She confidently stated. "Yes, it’s when someone is treated badly just for being different—because of their skin color, how they look, or what they believe in."

“That’s right, Jazzy,” Grandma announced.

Zaria’s eyes grew wide with pride for her big cousin’s correct answer. “Yay, Jazzy!” Zaria shouted.

“Around 1963 to 1965, there were a lot of protests regarding the Voting Rights of Blacks, especially in the Southern states. Many families were being harmed and treated poorly in the South, so the people were trying everything they could to register to vote to improve their living conditions.”

Refocusing on Jazzy, Grandma said, “Now, Jazzy, I know, you know some of this history. Zaria, I want you to listen well and try to remember what I’m telling you about your family, okay?” Zaria’s eyes sparkled as she perked up for her assignment, “Okay, Grandma.”

“I want you both to understand just how important it is to exercise your right to vote and always to be willing to do what is necessary to protect this right. In 1870, five years after the Civil War ended, Black Americans earned their right to vote. Congress adopted the 15th Amendment to the Constitution, guaranteeing the right to vote to Black men of voting age. Black women, along with all other women, were allowed to vote later in 1920.”

“Wait!” Jazzy’s hand flew up. “Why weren’t the women allowed to vote?”

“Women were considered second-class citizens back then. That’s another story that we’ll discuss at a later date.”

“Grandma, please don’t forget to discuss this later,” Jazzy stated.

“I won’t.” Grandma nodded to her new task.

“Because of the 15th Amendment, Selma elected its first Black congressman, city councilmen, and a criminal court judge. However, in 1876, the U.S. Supreme Court and many state courts narrowed the scope of the 15th Amendment. They said it did not always guarantee the right to vote. Soon, Black men began to lose their voting rights, especially in the South. Black voters were disenfranchised.” Grandma quickly raised an eyebrow at Jazzy.

BABY VOTE
VOTING IS PEOPLE POWER
WE DEMAND
VOTING RIGHTS
NOW!
LET MY PEOPLE VOTE

Jasmine shook her head while raising her hands. "No, Grandma, I do not know what disenfranchised means, but I can look it up real quick."

"No need, Jazzy." Grandma giggled, knowing how her granddaughter loved educating herself.

"To be disenfranchised means that a person or group of people loses the right to vote. In the South, voter registrars were given the power to prevent Black people from registering to vote in any way they could."

"That's not fair," Jasmine yelled as Zaria cosigned, "Yeah, not fair."

"Even after the passage of the Civil Rights Act of 1964, most African Americans in the southern United States were still unable to vote because of registration requirements, such as literacy tests and slow registration processes. Literacy is the ability to read and is not a requirement to vote in the United States. However, these literacy tests did not even test their reading ability."

"Wait," Jasmine held up the universal stop sign. "A person doesn't have to be able to read, and they can still vote?" She cringed.

"That's right. The important part of this is that the registrars only made Black people prove they could read, not White people," Grandma strongly stated.

"Oh, that's not right," Jazzy said.

"Some of the tests they would have to pass included reciting the Constitution, explaining a section of it, and guessing the number of jelly beans in a jar. If they failed at any one of the unfair tests, they would not be allowed to register to vote." Grandma sternly eyed Jazzy, "Now what does guessing jelly beans have to do with voting?"

"Nothing," Jazzy said.

"If these tests did not discourage them, the intimidation by the police, threats of being fired from their jobs, denial of credit, threats of eviction, and verbal abuse from White voting clerks also prevented Black southerners from voting. If Black voters passed a literacy test, they were often forced to pay a poll tax, which could take up most of their yearly income. Finally, after the tests had been passed and the poll tax paid, Black people had to find a registered voter willing to say they were good people and would make fine voters. Most voters in the South were White and would not do this.

Jazzy interrupted, "That's ridiculous."

"So, as a result, very few Black people were able to vote. They were fired from their jobs and received death threats just for trying to register to vote. By 1965, there were counties in Alabama where not a single Black person had voted for more than fifty years."

"Fifty years? Why didn't they fight?" Jazzy said sadly. Zaria, looking up at her cousin, yelled, "Yeah, fight, Grandma!"

"They had been trying to do that by marching to the courthouses, but they were beaten and threatened if they tried to vote. In Selma, Alabama, it seemed to be worse than in other southern states."

"Why Selma, Grandma?" Jazzy asked.

"I don't know the answer to that question. Maybe you can research that?"

"I think I will," Jazzy nodded.

"In another town near Selma, called Marion, a young Black man, an army veteran, Jimmie Lee Jackson, was shot in the stomach by a state trooper as he rushed to protect his mother and grandfather from being attacked, during a peaceful protest. Jackson died in Selma's Good Samaritan Hospital eight days later."

"A state trooper is the police, right?" Jazzy whispered.

"Yes," Grandma answered.

"Did they think he was trying to steal something?" Jazzy asked.

"No! Just another peaceful march to gain equal rights," Grandma firmly stated.

"The Dallas County Voting League was a group of people working hard to help Black citizens get registered to vote. In December 1964, Amelia Boynton of the Voters League wrote Dr. Martin Luther King, Jr. and the Southern Christian Leadership Conference (SCLC), asking them to help with their voting rights campaign. Jazzy, I know you have heard of Martin Luther King, Jr., right?"

"We learned about Martin Luther King when I was younger," she announced proudly.

"As you know," eyeing Jazzy, "Martin Luther King Jr. was a preacher from Atlanta, Georgia, who helped lead the country into social change for the betterment of all people.

Martin Luther King came to Selma to work with John Lewis, Rev. F.D. Reese, and many others to change the mistreatment of Blacks and help them get the same rights to vote as White Americans. It wasn't just in Selma, Alabama, where Black Americans were discouraged from voting, but in many places all over the United States of America. However, in Selma, many Black protestors were being beaten while trying to get the voting laws changed. The SCLC group was aware of Dallas County's sheriff, Jim Clark's, violent ways, but agreed to come to Selma, despite the danger, to assist with getting the voting laws changed. This would not only change the voting laws in the southern states but also in all states that discouraged Blacks from voting."

This time, Jazzy raised her hand as if she were in class. "Grandma, is this like voter suppression? This was a topic in school last year."

"Yes, but to the tenth power," Grandma stated and continued.

"In January of 1965, Martin Luther King held a mass meeting in Selma, declaring: 'We are going to bring a voting bill into the streets of Selma, Alabama.' Demonstrators were to walk from Brown Chapel AME, to the Dallas County courthouse. There, they would register to vote. That was the plan."

Grandma shook her head. "However, Clark met the protesters with violence. The front pages of national newspapers carried photos of him mistreating the demonstrators. He shoved Amelia Boynton half a block down to a patrol car and beat hotel manager Annie Lee Cooper in the head with his billy club. Clark struck the Rev. C.T. Vivian and broke his finger."

"Oh no!" Zaria blurted.

"Just a month later, in February, Clark and his men rounded up a group of children who were standing in protest in front of the courthouse, and forced them to run five miles to a prison camp outside of town. Several youngsters told newsmen later that the sheriff's men had used the nightsticks and cattle prods on them. Clark said he had not seen anything like that."

"He was even mean to the children?" Jazzy asked.

"Yes. He didn't care." Grandma continued, "There were other times, teenagers marched in support of their parents, and he had them arrested."

Jazzy shook her head, "Grandma, this man was doing way too much."

Grandma said, "Yep, however, Clark's evil actions strengthened the determination of the Selma marchers and drew the attention of the rest of the nation."

"What did the nation do to help these people?" Jazzy asked.

Grandma, patted her chest and said softly, "Our people. Many of those people were your family members."

A sadness crossed Jasmine's face. "Our family?"

"Yes, you guys remember cousin Renda in Alabama?"

The girls nodded yes. Zaria blurted with pride, "I know cousin Renda."

"Her mother, we called Big Auntie, was right behind Amelia when she was pushed in front of the courthouse." The girls' mouths fell open in astonishment.

"Uncle Sonny and cousin Horace both had marched for the right to vote. Your uncle Sonny was only about sixteen or seventeen years old when he was thrown in jail for participating in a peaceful march."

"Our uncle Sonny?" Zaria began to tear up. She understood more than Grandma thought she did.

"Come here, sweetie. It's okay. That was a long time ago, and Uncle Sonny is fine. You know why?"

"Why?" Zaria cried.

"Because God was protecting us then as He protects us now. You remember I told you that I always ask God to protect my family?" Zaria nodded. "I learned to pray and have faith in God from my parents, your Papa and Granny."

"Oh, okay." Zaria returned to her seat on the floor with her cousin.

"I know this is a lot of information, but now we are getting into the meat of this story as far as your great-great-granddaddy's heroism is concerned," Grandma said.

"It was Jimmy Lee Jackson's death that sparked the idea of a march from Selma to Montgomery to demand equal voting rights. Marchers wanted to pressure Alabama Governor George Wallace to guarantee Black people the right to vote in his state."

Jazzy and Zaria watched their grandma tell the story as if they were sitting around a campfire listening to a suspenseful tale of a legendary monster.

"I was told, on the day Martin Luther King came to speak to the people in Selma, hundreds of people flooded the narrow streets. The excitement and feeling of hope gleamed across their faces as they entered Brown Chapel to be led by Martin Luther King. King and the other groups planned a non-violent march from Selma to the capitol in Montgomery, Alabama, a fifty-four-mile trail, to speak to the governor of Alabama, George Wallace. King did not join the marchers for the first march. He had heard the Judge would stop the protestors by any means, so he stayed back to find more support from ministers and leaders around the country." Grandma took in a deep breath as she continued.

"On March 7, 1965, the people of Selma and other supporter groups gathered at Brown Chapel Church to begin the journey, led by John Lewis and Hosea Williams. As the protestors marched and sang songs of inspiration, many wondered what this day would bring.

Change for the better? More pain? Or worse?" Concern grew across Grandma's face.

"There was a girl, named Sheyann Webb, who was nine years old, the youngest marcher that day. Known as the youngest Freedom Fighter."
"Nine? She was younger than me?" Jazzy cried out.

"Yes," Grandma answered. "You should look her up and get her book."

"She wrote a book, too?" Jazzy shouted.

"Yes, but I think she wrote it when she was a bit older. You can read about what she experienced as a little girl protesting for voting rights." Grandma smiled.

"When the marchers got to the top of the bridge, they could see Sheriff Clark and his men on the other side. About five hundred and twenty-five marchers crossed the Edmund Pettus Bridge. They were met by Sheriff Clark and his deputies, along with state troopers, who were ordered to stop the march by Governor George Wallace. Some were sitting high on their horses while others stood, but all wore combat helmets and gas masks, as if they were ready for war. 'This is an unlawful assembly, and you are ordered to disperse, go home, or go to your church. This march will not continue,' said Sheriff Jim Clark.

I'm sure most marchers thought they'd probably be taken to jail like before, but based on interviews, fear grew in the eyes of all when they noticed the war-like armor worn by the police. When the marchers did not turn around, police on foot and horseback began beating marchers with billy clubs, whips, and cattle prods."

"Cattle prods?" Jazzy asked.

"Cattle prods are sticks often used to control animals with electric shocks or poking to make them go in a specific direction," said Grandma.

"Oh," said Jazzy. Zaria switched her eyes toward her cousin without saying a word.

"They shot firehoses with enough pressure to knock down and bruise the marchers. Members of the posse attacked the marchers with weapons made of rubber tubing wrapped in barbed wire. In panic, fearing for their lives, marchers ran back across the bridge toward Brown Chapel and the surrounding neighborhood for safety, looking for anywhere to hide. Many people were seen dragging family and friends, bloody from the beatings, to shelter.

EDMUND PETTUS BRIDGE

The wounds ranged from broken teeth and severe head gashes to fractured ribs and wrists. John Lewis suffered a skull fracture, and Amelia Boynton was beaten unconscious. Many people were treated, and the most seriously injured were sent to the hospital overnight. After the commotion, many protesters were taken to jail. They had no money to pay for their release, so they remained in prison for days. This day is now known as Bloody Sunday."

"Grandma, this is a very sad story," said Jazzy.

"Yeah, Grandma, this is sad," cried Zaria.

"I know it is, but you need to know what your family went through so that you would have the same rights as others." Grandma sighed.

"Photos and television footage of Bloody Sunday became national news. This was a great thing because then Americans could not deny the violent racism they were witnessing in their own country. They were shocked by the acts of Clark and Wallace, and many became supporters of the Civil Rights Movement." Grandma smiled with satisfaction.

"King and other leaders encouraged these new supporters to come to Selma for a second march to Montgomery. King sent a telegram to religious leaders across the country asking them to join him in Selma. Many people of all races and spiritual backgrounds responded to him. President Lyndon Johnson had also called the violence that was happening in Alabama 'an American tragedy'."

"That was a lot, but I'm glad the rest of the world could see it," said Jazzy.

"You're right," Grandma stated.

"On Tuesday, March 9, just two days after Bloody Sunday, King, along with Ralph Abernathy, Andrew Young, and other leaders, led a second march to the Edmund Pettus Bridge. This time, there were about 1,500 marchers. King looked at the many officers standing in front of them, ready to stop them again by any means necessary. King turned to the other leaders before continuing. Then, they kneeled in prayer, rose, and led the marchers back across the bridge. He and the leaders knew that the only way they would reach Montgomery successfully was to have a better plan. The second march became more of a demonstration known as 'Turnaround Tuesday.'"

Grandma said, "Back to the drawing board."

Zaria looked confused. Jazzy said softly, "They had to make a new plan."

"The activists, community leaders, and Martin Luther King met again at Brown Chapel often to come up with a plan to get the marchers to Montgomery safely. While King spoke to the President of the United States to secure the National Guard's protection from the police, other leaders worked to organize rest stops for the marchers along the fifty-four-mile route. Most of the people in the city were sharecroppers, which meant they didn't own the land and couldn't give permission to others to use it. Others were too scared of retaliation from the sheriff and his deputies to offer their land."

"Wait!" Jazzy commanded, "The police would hurt the people if they just allowed the marchers to stay on their land? Aren't they supposed to assist good people who follow the law? These people weren't breaking the law, right, Grandma?"

"You're correct, Jazzy. The people were just giving them a place to rest. They just wanted to register to vote and have the same rights as White people." Zaria was smart and understood the gist of this conversation, but looked a bit confused.

"Remember, your great-great-grandfather, David Hall, worked as the manager of the George Washington Carver housing authority, which was right next to Brown Chapel. Although he wasn't in any of the marches, he felt that having the right to vote was very important.

He was a very proud man, and some of his family and friends had been hurt in these protests. So I'm sure he was quite angry about that.

When he found out about the need for a resting place for the marchers, he came forward or was asked, not sure which one, but I can imagine my granddaddy saying, 'I own my land, I'm not a sharecropper.' He had purchased his land more than twenty years ago. 'If you need to stay on my land for rest and food, you are more than welcome to do so.' Because he was that kind of man, he was a serious, hard-working man, and always with a purpose.

Cousin Horace said Granddaddy would say, 'Sleeping is for dreamers,' and 'Laziness will kill you.' That's where my daddy, your PaPa, got that way of talking in riddles from. Daddy said, granddaddy said, 'Just give a man enough rope and he'll hang himself.' Grandma laughed.

"By this time, March of 1965, his children were grown and had moved away to different cities and states, but visited often, so he told them not to visit him during this march. He didn't want his family to be hurt. Granddaddy's life was threatened. The stores and banks refused to give him credit so that he and his family would suffer, but he never gave in to the threats."

Grandma leaned in toward the girls, almost whispering and said, "Then one late night, the Ku Klux Klan circled Granddaddy's house on horses holding big fiery billy clubs, hoping to intimidate him so that he wouldn't allow the marchers to rest on his farm.

Granddaddy never backed down. He knew how to be self-sufficient, but more importantly, he knew God would protect him. He said in a newspaper interview later, 'I would just have to depend on my faith in God to protect us from any reprisals.'

His bravery was contagious; two other farm owners joined in and let the marchers rest on their land as well."

Jazzy's face twisted in a mix of fear and anger. "Did they want to kill our GG-grandaddy?"

Grandma softly announced, "There were rumors of some people wanting to hurt my granddaddy and the other landowners, but I do not have any details of that."

"Poor GG-granddaddy. He was just trying to help," Zaria said. "What happened then, Grandma?"

"Another march departed from Brown Chapel AME Church on March 21, 1965. The supporters had grown from 1,500 to over 3,000. This time, the marchers had the National Guard protecting them as they began the third and final journey from Selma to Montgomery, the capitol of Alabama. Jazzy, you're too young to remember my grandmother, Juanita Henderson, your granny, and Uncle Sonny's mother, but she marched to Granddaddy Hall's farm, too. However, some of the senior citizens were driven back to Selma after completing the first leg of the march."

"We had a lot of our family in this movement."

"You're right, Jazzy–this movement that changed the world," said Grandma.

"No-no, Kai." A voice screamed from the other room.

"Uh-oh, Kai is up," Zaria warned. "No more story time."

Kai, the baby boy, was very energetic and curious. Big sister Zaria knew he was not in the habit of sitting still for stories.

Kai ran into the room, with Daddy not too far behind.

"Okay, Kai, I need you to sit down for story time. Play with your blocks while I finish the story, okay?" Grandma sternly suggested.

Grandma thought this was an excellent opportunity to discuss the songs.

"Back to the story. The marchers sang songs, freedom songs, while they marched, which I imagined kept their spirits up through these trying times."

"What song, Grandma?" Zaria blurted.

Grandma started singing:

"Ain't gonna let nobody turn me around
Turn me around, turn me around,
Ain't gonna let nobody turn me around
I'm gonna keep on walkin', keep on talkin',
Marchin' up that freedom land.
Ain't gonna let no jailhouse turn me around
Turn me around, turn me around,
Ain't gonna let no jailhouse turn me around
I'm gonna keep on walkin', keep on talkin',
Marchin' up that freedom land.
Ain't gonna let injustice turn me around
Turn me around, turn me around,
Ain't gonna let injustice turn me around
I'm gonna keep on walkin', keep on talkin',
Marchin' up that freedom land.
Ain't gonna let nobody turn me around
Turn me around, turn me around,
Ain't gonna let nobody turn me around
I'm gonna keep on walkin', keep on talkin',
Marchin' up that freedom land."

Both girls, along with Kai, were bobbing back and forth as Grandma sang, joining in the chorus.

"There were many songs led by the Freedom Riders during the fifty-four mile journey, but I think this was the most popular one."

"I like it. I think I'll make some beats for it," Jazzy smiled. She enjoyed making music on her computer.

"I know you'll make great music to add to the lyrics."

“Granddaddy’s farm was the first stop of the journey. When they arrived, they found four large tents, each equipped with sleeping bags, supplies, and first aid. One tent was for the men, one for the women, another for reporters, and the last for the Civil Rights leaders, activists, and religious leaders.”

“They had to sleep outside in tents? Wasn’t it cold?” Jazzy asked.

"Yes, it was very cold. The marchers made fires for warmth by adding wood to Granddaddy's oil cans. There was nothing pleasant or comfortable about this march, even with the rest areas. But the Selmians and supporters had to keep fighting the 'good fight', so that they, as well as future Black Americans, would have the same voting rights as White Americans. Voting is Power!"

Jazzy nodded, "Yeah, they needed some power."

"Yes, sweetie, we all still need that kind of power," Grandma agreed.

"The last march was successful because three kind citizens opened their land to the marchers, giving them a safe place to rest before completing their long journey to Montgomery. Your great-great-grandfather was the first campsite, which is now a national historic site, the David Hall Farm.

The second family was the Steele family, and the third was the Gardner family, who were also threatened by the people who were against Blacks voting in the South. Granddaddy Hall took a courageous stand as he risked everything to join in the fight for Blacks to have the same rights as Whites to vote."

Jazzy smiled with pride, while Zaria cheered, "Yay, GG-granddaddy."

"Over twenty-four thousand people arrived at the Alabama state capitol on March 25, 1965. Everyone was thrilled to have finally reached the Capitol. This is where Dr. King gave his famous speech, 'How Long? Not Long.' Jazzy, you should look up that speech."

"I will. We learned about some of this in class, but I don't remember learning about all of this violence." Jazzy sighed.

"I know. Unfortunately, I have more violence to share. On the evening of the 25th, there was a lady named Viola Liuzzo, who had come from Detroit to Alabama to support the voting rights movement, who was killed by Ku Klux Klan members while taking marchers back to Selma from Montgomery. Remember, the men circling your GG-Granddaddy's house?"

Both girls nodded, quietly stating, "Yes."

"Those men were from the same group. These were dangerous times with dangerous people. However, due to the powerful impact of the marches in Selma, the Voting Rights Act of 1965 was presented to Congress on March 17, 1965. President Johnson signed the bill into law on August 6, 1965."

"Thank Goodness," shouted Jazzy.

David Hall is a name you two should never forget because he was an ordinary man who did an extraordinary thing, and your great-great-grandfather. Many unsung heroes demonstrated bravery beyond belief to help us have the right to vote today!"

"That was our GG-Grandaddy. YAY!" Zaria screamed.

Kai joined. "Yay!" he yelled, clapping and jumping up, not understanding what anyone was talking about, but he would in due time.

Jazzy looked at her grandma, announcing proudly, "I'm going to do my report on my great-great-granddaddy, David Hall. Grandma, will you help me gather all the information?"

Grandma's work was done here.

"Nothing would make me happier. Let's get started."

I can't express the pride that fills our family's heart when we think of the heroic steps our daddy, granddaddy, and great-granddaddy took to support this historic event that changed the world.

This book is dedicated to my three beautiful grandchildren, Jasmine Richards, Zaria Scott, and Kai Scott.

And those dear to my heart who have moved on:
Rest in peace, my angels: my loving parents, Abner and Nettie Hall, Aunt Susie "Sweet" Hall, Uncle Johnny Hall, Aunt Dorothy Maiden, and cousin Horace French.

About The Author

Michele L. Waters was born and raised in Southern California and now resides in Georgia. Waters recently retired from a 40-year career in Diagnostic Imaging. Over the years, she has published three books, including Through the Eyes of My Mulatto Daughter, which was a Finalist in the National Indie Excellence Awards for Multicultural Fiction. This title is also featured as a required reading in one of the Diversity classes at Towson University. When not writing, Michele enjoys travelling, reading, and playing with her grandchildren, which has inspired her to write her first children's book, America's Unsung Hero....Our Hero.

About The Illustrator

Janine Carrington (pronouns she/her) is a Black artist of Caribbean heritage who specializes in Black affirming children's books and comics. Born in Toronto, Ontario and taught the basics of drawing by her father, she went on to study art in high school and at the Ontario College of Art and Design. She spent her last year of college in Florence, Italy, and traveled extensively to countries of the African diaspora. She has been working professionally since 2008 for herself and with authors and educators to create art that uplifts all children, especially those of colour.

GLOSSARY

Bravery - the state of showing mental or moral strength to face danger, difficulty, or fear." Contrary to popular belief, bravery isn't the absence of fear; it is taking action and proceeding forward despite the presence of fear.

Sharecropping - Black families and some poor white families would rent small plots of land to work themselves; in return, they would give a large portion of their earnings to the landowner to cover the cost of supplies and rent. This system kept blacks indebted to white landowners and made it very difficult for blacks to own their land.

Voter registrars, **also known as election registrars** - Individuals responsible for registering people to vote.

Ku Klux Klan - In the 1960s, the Ku Klux Klan was a decentralized collection of white supremacist terrorist organizations dedicated to violently opposing the Civil Rights Movement and maintaining segregation.

Civil Rights - personal rights guaranteed and protected by the U.S. Constitution and federal laws enacted by Congress.

15th Amendment to the Constitution - The amendment states that the right to vote shall not be denied or abridged on account of race, color, or previous condition of servitude.

Disenfranchised means that a person or group of people loses the right to vote. Disenfranchisement happened in many ways.

Billy club - A heavy club, usually made of wood, carried by police officers. However, its meaning and symbolism extended far beyond a simple tool, becoming associated with police brutality and the suppression of the Civil Rights Movement.

Cattle Prod - A handheld, stick-like device, often electrified, used by farmers and ranchers to direct, herd, or control livestock like cattle by delivering a mild, low-current electric shock or by poking. It serves to motivate animals to move in a desired direction from a safe distance, protecting the handler from physical harm.

SNCC - The Student Nonviolent Coordinating Committee (SNCC) was a key student-led organization in the American Civil Rights Movement, formed in 1960 to coordinate and amplify student-led protests against racial segregation and discrimination.

SNLC - Southern Christian Leadership Conference (SNLC) The two main goals of the SCLC are to fight for equal rights for Black Americans and to defend the rights of all Americans (all people).

References:

Abner Hall

Ronald Hall

Mary McGuire

Susie Hall

Ceola Gaylor

Alma Thornton

Horace French

Johnny Hall

William (Sonny) Henderson

Mildred McGuire

Claire Haughey

Alabama Department of Public Safety

Associated Press News

AP Photo file

Photos by Bill Hudson AP

Photos by Bruce Hartford

Photos by John Kouns

Photos by Spider Martin

The Bloody Sunday Events of 1965. Selma to Montgomery

March - Selma – Montgomery March 1965 (Full Version)

www.ingramcontent.com/pod-product-compliance
Lightning Source LLC
LaVergne TN
LVHW070222110826
845147LV00003B/626

* 9 7 8 0 9 8 2 8 6 7 0 9 9 *